MUNTHE'S CAPRI

A Pictorial Biography by Bengt Jangfeldt

HYLAEA

Translated from the Swedish
by Harry D. Watson

© Bengt Jangfeldt 2004
Layout Fredrika Siwe
Printed by Fälth & Hässler, Värnamo 2005
ISBN 91-971447-6-2

Contents

A Nordic Dream

Capri is mentioned for the first time by the Greek historian Strabo at the end of the first century BC, but not until Roman times does the island really enter the historical record. When Octavian (later the Emperor Augustus) made landfall on Capri in 29 BC on his way from Egypt, he was so delighted by the island that he acquired it from the Neapolitans in exchange for its neighbouring island of Ischia. In later years he often stayed on Capri, and several of the island's ruins can be assigned to his time.

Augustus's warm feelings for Capri were inherited by his stepson Tiberius, who moved there permanently in 26 AD and remained for eleven years, till his death in the year 37. Tiberius had several large villas built, one of which is a well-preserved ruin: the Villa Jovis, or Jupiter Villa, on the eastern tip of the island.

Even if no more emperors settled on Capri, the island remained in the possession of the imperial family, as far as we know, until the end of the 5th century, when it was incorporated with Sorrento, which was subject to the Duchy of Naples. The island was constantly under threat from Saracen pirates from north Africa and at the beginning of the 12th century it was invaded by the Normans (descendants of Vikings from Normandy), who had already subjected Sicily and southern Italy. After belonging in turn to the kings of Anjou and Aragon in the 13th, 14th and 15th centuries, control passed to Spain at the beginning of the 16th century. In addition to the threat from Moorish pirates, there were now attacks by the expanding Ottoman empire. In 1535 Capri was invaded and ravaged by the Turkish admiral Kheir-ed-Din, whose nickname Barbarossa (Red Beard) was to be applied to the castle in Anacapri, the town in the upper part of the island.

From 1734 onwards, with occasional intervals, the Spanish Bourbon kings ruled over Naples and the Two Sicilies. During the Napoleonic Wars power vacillated between the French and the British. From 1806 until 1815, it was France which ruled. But after the defeat at Waterloo the governance of Capri reverted to king Ferdinand IV. When Italy was united in 1861, the people of Capri and Naples voted by a large majority to be incorporated into the new kingdom.

Italian unification meant among other things that new railway lines were opened, joining the country to the rest of Europe. As a result, the Capri which Axel Munthe had first visited in 1876 became, after barely a decade, a tempting and accessible destination. However, most of those who visited the island were not tourists, but rather individuals who wished to indulge their private and professional interests: authors, artists, historians, archaeologists, people hungry for learning in the broadest sense of the word.

*

Axel Munthe, the son of a chemist, was born at Oskarshamn in 1857 and grew up in Vimmerby and Stockholm. After completing a preparatory degree in medicine at Uppsala University in 1876, he was sent in the autumn of that same year to Menton on the French Riviera for the sake of his lungs. It was in this connection that he visited Capri for the first time.

This photograph of a very young Axel Munthe was taken in Naples during one of his first visits to the city — perhaps in 1876, when he also visited Capri for the first time.

In the introductory lines to The Story of San Michele, Munthe describes his first encounter with Capri in the following manner: »I sprang from the Sorrento sailing-boat on to the little beach. Swarms of boys were playing about among the upturned boats or bathing their shining bronze bodies in the surf, and old fishermen in red Phrygian caps sat mending their nets outside their boat-houses.«

PRI - Marina.

What was it that persuaded the young medical student to take himself off to Capri as soon as he had left Sweden? In northern Europe, including Sweden, romantic notions of Italy flourished, and not unnaturally they inspired Axel Munthe too. But why Capri in particular?

During the 1850s the book *Wanderjahre in Italien* by Ferdinand Gregorovius, the German expert on Italy, appeared, with the chapter on Capri published separately in 1868. Whether it was Gregorovius who awakened Munthe's interest in the island, or whether he read the book only later, is impossible to say. But there is no doubt that he did know of it. A phrase in one of Munthe's travel sketches from 1885 – that the poets had compared Capri to »a dreaming sphinx or an antique sarcophagus« – was taken almost word for word from Gregorovius's book.

Whatever the inspiration looked like, this first visit resulted in a love affair between Munthe and Capri which would last throughout his life.

In 1880 Axel Munthe gained his doctoral degree in medicine in Paris, and during the next decade he practised as a doctor in the French capital. But he longed for Italy and travelled there as often as he could. The next time he returned to Capri it was in company with his young wife Ultima.

Ferdinand Gregorovius's book about Capri was illustrated by the German artist Lindemann-Frommel. Here we see the Bay of Naples and the old road to Anacapri. Mount Barbarossa, on the left, would later be acquired by Axel Munthe. The drawing was made in 1865, eleven years before Munthe set foot on Capri for the first time.

They married in November 1880 and spent the winter of 1880-81 on the island. During this stay, Munthe worked as a doctor and was awarded the Italian Order of the Crown for his efforts during a typhus epidemic on Capri and an earthquake on Ischia.

However, when he wished to visit Capri during the cholera epidemic in Naples in the autumn of 1884, he was not allowed to go ashore because of the risk of infection. He had more success in the summer of 1885, and the reception was enthusiastic: »One felt proud to be a fellow-Swede when one went ashore on Capri,« wrote his travelling companion Mathilda Cederlund: »Everyone embraced him, old men, old women, young people, children — all of them were happy to see him again, people of rank as much as the poor people.«

When Munthe returned to Capri in January 1888 it was in sombre mood, as his marriage to Ultima had collapsed. This time he stayed on the island for a year and a half. He rented a house in Anacapri from the French artist Édouard Sain. In the autumn of 1889 he moved to Rome, where during the 1890s he made an illustrious career as a doctor. But his heart remained in Capri, and before he left the island he took out a ten-year lease on another house in Anacapri, the Villa Damecuta.

However, he dreamt of one day acquiring a house of his own on the island, and thanks to the considerable income generated by his medical practice in Rome, he was able to translate his dream into reality. In 1895 he bought an old house on Capodimonte in Anacapri, with a ravishing view over the Bay of Naples and the Sorrento peninsula. On the foundations of Master Vincenzo's house, Munthe raised a villa which was named San Michele. He also acquired the surrounding land, including the hill behind the villa with Barbarossa's fortress. The genesis of the villa is imaginatively described in *The Story of San Michele*.

Munthe had weak eyes and suffered from the intense sunlight on Capodimonte. Therefore, as early as 1902 he bought another property, Torre di Materita, on a shadier part of the island. It was this old Saracen tower that served as Munthe's real home on Capri, while the Villa San Michele was let for long periods. With the passing of the years Axel Munthe became the owner of several other pieces of real estate in Anacapri and came to acquire a unique position on the island. In 1914 he was proclaimed an honorary citizen.

From 1893 Axel Munthe worked as physician to Crown Princess Victoria of Sweden-Norway – from 1907, the queen of Sweden – and in 1903 he was appointed physician-in-ordinary. The relationship between Munthe and his patient was significantly more intimate than that which is dictated by the Hippocratic oath, and it lasted for thirty-seven years, until the queen's death in 1930. When Munthe gave up his medical practice in Rome in 1901 and moved to Capri for good, Victoria followed him. During the first years she stayed in hotels in Anacapri, from 1909 in a villa of her own, Casa Caprile. As a result of Munthe's and Victoria's long presence in Anacapri, the island had, for several decades, a markedly Swedish stamp.

Axel Munthe lived on Capri for a good forty years. In the autumn of 1943, when he was about to go back to Italy after his accustomed summer holiday in Sweden, his return journey was hindered by the progress of the war – Allied troops had landed in southern Italy. Munthe remained in Sweden, where he died six years later in the Royal Palace.

*

This book sets out to describe Axel Munthe's Capri in pictures — the houses he owned and lived in, the people and animals he associated with. The narrative spans almost seventy years. It is impossible to imagine Axel Munthe without Capri, but it is almost equally difficult to imagine Capri without Munthe. No-one has sung the praises of this Mediterranean island with the same love and passion as he did; no-one in modern times has done more for Capri's reputation and popularity. *The Story of San Michele*, published in millions of copies in about forty languages, has made the island internationally known in a manner unprecedented since the days of Augustus and Tiberius. And in the form of the Villa San Michele, a living witness to one man's vision and works, Munthe's efforts on behalf of Capri continue long after his death.

Crown Princess Victoria's photograph shows Anacapri's main street (now the Via G. Orlandi), where it runs into what is now Anacapri's nodal point for buses and taxis — Piazza Victoria. The pine-trees, which are said to have been saved from felling on one occasion by Axel Munthe, remained untouched until March 2004, when the one on the right, which had begun to rot, was chopped down.

A priest outside Hermann Moll's wine-shop in Ana-capri, where Munthe used to buy his wines. (Photo Crown Princess Victoria 1903)

Women in Anacapri are greeted by Crown Princess Victoria's poodle Tom outside Dr. Vincenzo Cuomo's villa. The famous pines in the piazza can be seen in the background. (Photo Crown Princess Victoria 1903)

Next page: Crown Princess Victoria enjoyed visiting the towns along the Amalfi coast. Here, her camera has captured Munthe during an excursion to Ravello around the year 1900.

The Villa

Axel Munthe had always dreamt of a place of his own on Capri. In 1895 he bought the house of the carpenter Vincenzo Alberino and the ruins of a church called after the archangel Michael.

»I have been lucky enough to buy an old church situated on the loveliest point of the island all for myself and I am now busy fitting it up as a dwelling-house,« Munthe wrote in a letter of 1896 – »it is surrounded by a vineyard and it covers one of Tiberius's palaces, a good deal of which I have excavated, finding in the process many antiquities and hundreds of Roman and Greek coins. The church was formerly a temple of Isis, then became a part of Tiberius's palace (I have excavated a room with mosaic floor and frescoes from his time), and later again a temple dedicated to St. Michael. It was destroyed by the Saracen Barbarossa in 1560, became a fortress in 1804, when Britain occupied Capri; it was stormed by the French in 1806 (it dominated what was then the only road to Capri), then it was turned into a powder magazine, and now it is my home.«

However, Munthe soon abandoned his plans to use the church as a dwelling and instead turned his hand to rebuilding Alberino's house and workshop.

The first version of the villa seems to have been finished in 1897. There was a kitchen and a dining-room on the lower floor, and the upper floor contained a study and a bedroom – together with a terrace covered by a pergola, a typical feature for Capri, which was left over from Master Vincenzo's house. During the next phase, the terrace was built in and converted into a new bedroom. The Villa San Michele is »a creation of the most fantastic beauty, poetry and inutility I have ever seen clustered together,« commented Henry James in a letter in June 1899.

In the story »The Saint's Afternoon«, James wrote that »here above all had the thought and the hand come from far away – even from *Ultima Thule*, and yet were in possession triumphant and acclaimed. Well, all one could say was that the way they had felt their opportunity, the divine conditions

The chapel with the Barbarossa fortress, photographed by Crown Princess Victoria in 1903.

Mastro Vincenzo's house as it looked at the time when Munthe acquired it. The photograph was taken behind the house (where the cypress alley planted by Munthe begins) and shows the entrance to the upper floor. Under the little window can be seen the bow-shaped opening to the staircase which joined — and still joins — the upper and lower floors. (Ca. 1895)

Mastro Vincenzo's door- and window-design was largely adopted by Munthe but modified and made more aesthetically pleasing. Crown Princess Victoria's photograph shows that Munthe converted the left-hand door-opening into a window in the Venetian style. (1903)

of the place, spoke of the advantage of some such intellectual perspective as a remote original standpoint alone perhaps can give. If what had finally, with infinite patience, passion, labour, taste, got itself done there, was like some supreme reward of an old dream of Italy, something perfect after long delays, was it not verily in *Ultima Thule* that the vow would have been piously enough made and the germ tenderly enough nursed?«

At this time the villa had not yet been named after the archangel Michael, but was called the Villa Tiberiana after the emperor Tiberius.

Despite Henry James's enthusiasm, Munthe was dissatisfied with the villa's design. »I told Mastro Nicola,« he writes in *The Story of San Michele*, »that the proper way to build one's house was to knock everything down never mind how many times and begin again until your eye told you that everything was right. The eye knew much more about architecture than

On the following pages Munthe's villa is portrayed in its different building phases: the first version of the villa (photo Esposito); the second, with its integral roof-terrace (photographed in the summer of 1901 by Prince Max of Baden); and the third and final version, with the extension in the middle of the house (photo Crown Princess Victoria 1903).

did the books. The eye was infallible, as long as you relied on your own eye and not on the eye of other people.«

The Villa San Michele acquired its final form with the addition of a third floor with two guestrooms which was built onto the middle of the house.

In *The Story of San Michele* Munthe claims that he does not really know how the transformation took place, but we know that he had professional help from the Italian architect Aristide Sartorio.

The panoramic photo on the preceding two pages with Munthe's villa and the exceptional view of the Sorrento peninsula were taken by Crown Princess Victoria from the Hotel Molaro (the present Hotel San Michele) 1903.

The Miracle of Sant'Antonio

SANT'ANTONIO had done another miracle. I was living in a little contadino house in Anacapri, whitewashed and clean with a sunny pergola outside the open windows and friendly, simple people all around me. Old Maria Porta-Lettere, La Bella Margherita, Annarella and Gioconda were all delighted to see me back amongst them. Don Dionisio's Capri Bianco was better than ever and it dawned upon me more and more that the parroco's Capri Rosso was equally good. From sunrise till sunset I was hard at work in what had been Mastro Vincenzo's garden, digging the foundations of the huge arches of the loggia outside my future home. Mastro Nicola and his three sons were digging by my side and half-a-dozen girls with laughing eyes and swinging hips were carrying away the earth in huge baskets on their heads. A yard below the surface we had come upon the Roman walls, opus reticulatum as hard as granite with nymphs and bacchantes dancing on the intonaco of Pompeian red. Below appeared the mosaic floor framed with vine-leaves of nero antico and a broken pavement of beautiful palombino now in the centre of the big loggia. A fluted column of cipollino, now supporting the little loggia in the inner courtyard, lay across the pavement where it had fallen two thousand years ago, crushing in its fall a big vase of Parian marble, the lion-headed handle of which is now lying on my table.

None of my fellow-workers could read or write, none had ever worked at the building of any other houses than those of contadini, all more or less alike. But Mastro Nicola knew how to build an arch as did his father and his grandfather from untold generations, the Romans had been their masters. That this was going to be a different house from any they had ever seen before, had already dawned upon them, they were all tremendously interested, nobody knew so far what it was going to look like, nor did I. All we had to go by was a rough sort of sketch drawn by myself with a piece of charcoal on the white garden-wall, I cannot draw anything, it looked as if drawn by the hand of a child.

»This is my house,« I explained to them, »with huge Roman columns supporting its vaulted rooms and of course small Gothic columns in all the windows. This is the loggia with its strong arches, we will decide by and by how many arches there will be. Here comes a pergola, over a hundred columns, leading up to the chapel, never mind the public road running straight across my pergola now, it will have to go. Here looking out on Castello Barbarossa comes another loggia, I do not quite see what it looks like for the present, I am sure it will spring out of my head at the right moment. This is a small inner court, all white marble, a sort of atrium with a cool fountain in its midst and heads of Roman Emperors in niches round the walls. Here behind the house we are going to knock down the garden-wall and build a cloister something like the Lateran cloister in Rome. Here comes a large terrace where all you girls will dance the tarantella on summer evenings. On the top of the garden we shall blast away the rock and build a Greek theatre open on all sides to sun and wind. This is an avenue of cypresses leading up to the chapel which we will of course rebuild as a chapel with cloister stalls and stained-glass windows, I intend to make its my library. This is a colonnade with twisted Gothic columns surrounding the chapel and here looking out over the bay of Naples we are going to hoist an enormous Egyptian sphinx of red granite, older than Tiberius himself. It is the very place for a sphinx. I do not see for the present where I shall get it from but I am sure it will turn up in time.«

The whole garden was full of thousands and thousands of polished slabs of coloured marble, africano, pavonazetto, giallo antico, verde antico, cipollino, alabastro, all now forming the pavement of the big loggia, the chapel and some of the terraces. A broken cup of agate of exquisite shape, several broken and unbroken Greek vases, innumerable fragments of early Roman sculpture, including, according to Mastro Nicola, la gamba di Timberio, dozens of Greek and Roman inscriptions came to light as we were digging. While we were planting the cypresses bordering the little lane to the chapel, we came upon a tomb with a skeleton of a man, he had a Greek coin in his mouth, the bones are still there where we found them, the skull is lying on my writing-table.

The huge arcades of the big loggia rose rapidly out of the earth, one by one the hundred white columns of the pergola stood out against the sky.

What had once been Mastro Vincenzo's house and his carpenter workshop was gradually transformed and enlarged into what was to become my future home. How it was done I have never been able to understand, nor has anybody else who knows the history of the San Michele of to-day. I knew absolutely nothing about architecture, nor did any of my fellow-workers, nobody who could read or write ever had anything to do with the work, no architect was ever consulted, no proper drawing or plan was ever made, no exact measurements were ever taken. It was all done all'occhio as Mastro Nicola called it.

AXEL MUNTHE, The Story of San Michele

Anacapri's gravedigger Pasquale Alberino — called Pacciale in The Story of San Michele — and the lapdog Gioia, photographed by Crown Princess Victoria in front of the entrance to the Villa San Michele around the year 1900. »Old Pacciale had been a particular friend of mine for many years. In his early days he had been a coral-fisher like most of the male population of Capri in those days. After various vicissitudes he had ended by becoming the official gravedigger of Anacapri, a bad job in a place where nobody dies as long as he keeps clear of the doctor« (The Story of San Michele).

The hallway, where Munthe had installed an ingenious system for identifying visitors. »In the little hallway hang four verdigris-covered metal bells taken from the church,« wrote Alexandra Bildt, the wife of the Swedish ambassador to Rome, in her diary in 1902: »The servant has to ring them according to the category of visitor: the doctor sits up there and can hear from the ring what kind of visit he is about to get. Unbelievably crafty!« (Photo Prince Max of Baden 1901)

Pasquale Alberino's daughters Rosina and Giovannina, Munthe's servant-girls in Anacapri and Rome, photographed here by Munthe (1889?). »Giovannina and Rosina belonged to the San Michele household, better servants I have never had, light of hand and foot, singing the whole day at their work« (The Story of San Michele).

»At table we were served by the lovely Maria, Munthe's ward, who [...] is said not to be allowed to leave the house for fear of her being corrupted,« wrote Alexandra Bildt in her diary: »He pays her no wages; instead, she belongs to ›la famiglia‹ and gets from him everything she needs.« (Photo Prince Max of Baden 1901)

The dining-room with a sculpture of the Madonna and Swedish pewter artefacts from the 18th century. (Photo Crown Princess Victoria 1901-02)

The bedroom, photographed by Crown Princess Victoria. The window next to the bed was walled in later but remains on the outside and can be seen from the atrium. Behind the pillar something which seems to be a drapery. Later, Munthe built an alcove here. (1901-02)

The study with the head of the mythical Medusa, which Munthe, according to his own account, found at the bottom of the sea, but which possibly has a more prosaic provenance. (Photo Crown Princess Victoria 1901-02)

The atrium, previously Mastro Vincenzo's entrance-yard. In the middle stands a well from Roman times, the wall contains inscriptions in Latin and other antique fragments. The bronze heads in the niches are late replicas of antique originals — the one on the left portrays Augustus's wife Livia. The column which holds up the atrium's loggia was, according to Munthe, found in Mastro Vincenzo's vineyard. The dogs are Jallah, Munthe's Russian greyhound, and Lippo, who belonged to Prince Max of Baden (who took the photo in 1901).

The sculpture gallery,
photographed by Prince
Max of Baden 1901.

The gallery continues in a
bow-shaped pergola which
offers an enchanting view
over the Bay of Naples.
The photos on the following
double-spread were taken
by Crown Princess Victoria
1903.

Munthe with Victoria's fox-terrier Fellow in the newly-planted cypress alley, which runs from the villa to the chapel. According to Munthe, the saplings came from the Villa d'Este in Rome. (Photo Crown Princess Victoria 1901)

This early photograph by Crown Princess Victoria shows that the chapel wall was originally adorned with the so-called Etruscan sphinx. The choice of the sphinx as San Michele's foremost symbol may have been inspired by the German poet Jean Paul — one of Munthe's favourites — who actually compared Capri to a sphinx. (1899-1900)

The Sphinx

Looking down from the parapet on the island at my feet, I told Mastro Nicola that we were to begin at once the emplacement for the sphinx, there was no time to lose. Mastro Nicola was delighted, why didn't we fetch the sphinx at once, where was it now? I said it was lying under the ruins of the forgotten villa of a Roman Emperor somewhere on the mainland. It had been lying waiting for me there for two thousand years. A man in a red mantle had told me all about it the first time I looked out over the sea from the very spot where we now stood. So far I had only seen it in my dreams. I looked down on the little white yacht on the Marina under my feet and said I was quite sure I would find the sphinx at the right time. The difficulty would be to bring it across the sea, it was in fact far too heavy a cargo for my boat, it was all of granite and weighed I did not know how many tons. Mastro Nicola scratched his head and wondered who was going to drag it up to San Michele. He and I of course.

*

Hardly had I fallen asleep than I found myself standing, on a lonely plain strewn with debris of broken masonry, huge blocks of travertine and fragments of marbles half hidden by ivy, rosemary and wild honeysuckle, cistus and thyme. On a crumbling wall of opus reticulatum sat an old shepherd playing on the flute of Pan to his flock of goats. His wild, long-bearded face was scorched by sun and wind, his eyes were burning like fire under his bushy eyebrows, his lean emaciated body was shivering under his long blue cloak of a Calabrian shepherd. I offered him a little tobacco, he handed me a slice of fresh goat-cheese and an onion. I understood him with difficulty.

What was the name of this strange place?

It had no name.

Where did he come from?

From nowhere, he had always been here, this was his home.

When Prince Max and Princess Marie Louise of Baden visited San Michele in the summer of 1901, the Etruscan sphinx had been exchanged for the Egyptian one, here in company with the royal couple's dog Lippo. The Etruscan sphinx, here photographed by Crown Princess Victoria, was moved to the balustrade on the chapel terrace.

Where did he sleep?

He pointed with his long staff to a flight of steps under a tumbledown archway. I climbed down the steps hewn in the rock and stood in a dim, vaulted room. In the corner a straw mattress with a couple of sheepskins as bed cover. Suspended round the walls and from the ceiling bunches of dried onions and tomatoes, an earthenware jug of water on the rough table. This was his home, these were his belongings. Here he had lived his whole life, here he would lie down one day to die. In front of me opened a dark subterranean passage half filled with debris from the fallen roof. Where did it lead to?

He did not know, he had never been there. He had been told as a boy that it led to a cave haunted by an evil spirit who had lived there for thousands of years, in the shape of a huge werewolf who would devour any man who should approach his cave.

I lit a torch and groped my way down a flight of marble steps. The passage widened more and more, an ice-cold blast of air blew in my face. I heard an uncanny moan which made the blood freeze in my veins. Suddenly I stood in a large hall. Two huge columns of African marble still supported a part of the vaulted roof, two others lay across the mosaic floor wrenched from their pedestals by the grip of the earthquake. Hundreds of huge bats were hanging in black clusters round the walls, others were fluttering in wild flight round my head, blinded by the sudden light of the torch. In the midst of the hall crouched a huge granite sphinx, staring at me with stony, wide-open eyes…

I started in my sleep. The dream vanished. I opened my eyes, the day was breaking. Suddenly I heard the call of the sea, imperious, irresistible like a command. I sprang to my feet, flung myself into my clothes and rushed up to the parapet of the chapel to hoist the signal to the yacht to make ready for the start. A couple of hours later I boarded my boat with provisions for a week, coils of stout rope, pick-axes and spades, a revolver, all my available money, a bundle of torches of resinous wood, such as fishermen use for night fishing. A moment later we hoisted sail for the most stirring adventure of my life. The following night we dropped anchor in a lonely cove, unknown to all but a few fishermen and smugglers. Gaetano was to wait for me there with the yacht for a week and to run for shelter to the nearest port in case bad weather set in. We knew this dangerous coast well, with no safe anchorage for a hundred miles. I also knew its wonderful inland, once the Magna Graecia of the Golden Ages of Hellenic art and culture, now the most desolate province of Italy abandoned by man to malaria and earthquake.

Three days later I stood on the same lonely plain strewn with broken masonry and huge blocks of travertine and fragments of marbles half hidden under ivy-rosemary and wild honeysuckle, cistus and thyme. On the crumbling wall of opus reticulatum sat the old shepherd playing on his pipe to his flock of goats. I offered him a little tobacco, he handed me a slice of fresh goat-cheese and an onion. The sun had already gone down behind the mountains, the deadly mist of malaria was slowly creeping over the desolate plain. I told him I had lost my way, I dared not wander about alone in this wilderness, might I stay with him for the night?

He led the way to his underground sleeping-quarters I knew so well from my dream. I lay down on his sheepskins and fell asleep.

It is all too weird and fantastic to be translated into written words, you would besides not believe me if I tried to do so. I hardly know myself where the dream ended and where reality began. Who steered the yacht into this hidden, lonely cove? Who led my way across this trackless wilderness to the unknown ruins of Nero's villa? Was the shepherd of flesh and blood or was he not Pan himself who had come back to his favourite haunts of old to play the flute to his flock of goats?

Do not ask me any questions, I cannot tell you, I dare not tell you. You may ask the huge granite sphinx who lies crouching on the parapet of the chapel in San Michele. But you will ask in vain. The sphinx has kept her own secret for five thousand years. The sphinx will keep mine.

AXEL MUNTHE, *The Story of San Michele*

This panoramic photograph from the turn of the twentieth century shows Mount Barbarossa and the narrow road which leads to the Villa San Michele (Via Porta, nowadays the Viale Axel Munthe). The large house on the right is the Villa Le Scale. The Hotel Barbarossa, now a school called the Villa Rosa, can be seen in the background.

In 1903 Munthe moved to a new home in Anacapri, the Torre di Materita (see page 95). For several years he alternated between living there (in the winter) and in the Villa San Michele (in the summer), but after 1907 the villa was for the most part rented out. The first paying guest was an American called Mrs. Bodine. After her, San Michele was let to the eccentric marchioness Luisa Casati, who lived in the villa throughout the 1920s and turned Munthe's aesthetic concepts upside down. Black velvet draperies and curtains of gold lace were hung up, black mats and animals' heads were laid on the marble floors and Munthe's antiquities were removed to make way for the marchioness's ebony furniture. Munthe protested, but to no avail.

In the 1930s the villa was rented by the American ambassador in Rome and his wife, Mr. and Mrs. Garrett.

»La Casati« wearing one of her favourite throat coverings, a boa. On the right, her boudoir on the villa's top floor (which nowadays is called »Casa Oliv«).

»The chapel itself which had given its name to my home had at last become mine. It was to become my library. Fine old cloister stalls surrounded the white walls, in its midst stood a large refectory table laden with books and terra-cotta fragments« (The Story of San Michele). Photo Prince Max of Baden 1901.

The Visitors

The Villa San Michele was already attracting visitors while it was being built. The married artists Søren and Marie Krøyer were there in the summer of 1896, Oscar Wilde in October 1897 and the Swedish artist Gustaf Cederström the following year. On 13th June 1899 the world-renowned author Henry James was Munthe's guest during the annual celebration of Anacapri's patron saint St. Anthony. When the Swedish author and social reformer Ellen Key stayed with Munthe in 1901 she described the Villa San Michele as »a miracle of taste,« and in 1907 the poet Rainer Maria Rilke was equally enchanted by the villa and its owner.

Victoria also visited the villa in 1899, in company with Crown Princess Stéphanie of Austria. After Munthe gave up his medical practice in Rome in 1901 and settled permanently on Capri, her visits became more frequent. She was on Capri again in 1901 and in 1902, and from 1903 she spent lengthy periods in Anacapri almost yearly.

Through the Crown Princess, Munthe came into close contact with the upper class and higher aristocracy of Europe. In 1903 Victoria was visited by the queen of Portugal, the Crown Princess of Prussia and Count Zeppelin (the inventor of the airship). The following year Kaiser Wilhelm, Victoria's cousin, visited the Villa San Michele. In the autumn of 1903 Prince Eugen spent some time on the island and in the spring of 1905 his nephew Crown Prince Gustaf Adolf visited Capri with his fiancée Princess Margaret.

Recurrent visitors included Victoria's other cousin Prince Max of Baden and his young wife Marie Louise. Their visits are immortalised in a number of photographs.

In October 1897 Oscar Wilde visited Capri along with his friend Lord Alfred Douglas. Wilde had just served a prison sentence for homosexual immorality and not everybody wished to be seen in the couple's company. But Munthe had a liberal attitude to sexual deviation and invited them to his home. Wilde reported in a letter: »We both lunched with Dr Munthe, who has a lovely villa and is a great connoisseur of Greek things. He is a wonderful personality«

The photograph was taken in Naples, where Wilde and Douglas lived in the autumn of 1897.

During the first of her longer visits to Capri, in 1903 and 1904, Crown Princess Victoria stayed with her entourage in the Hotel Molaro, a few hundred metres from the Villa San Michele. The hotel — nowadays called San Michele — had remained uninhabited for several years and the little company had it entirely to themselves. The Crown Princess's lady-in-waiting recalled that the few items of furniture were thick with dust, and »many people would have been amazed to see how simply Her Majesty used to live there and how she enjoyed these unsophisticated, rustic circumstances«.

The neighbouring island of Ischia can be seen in the background. (Photo Crown Princess Victoria 1903)

From her window in the Hotel Molaro Victoria could photograph her beloved doctor's villa. (1903)

The Prince and Princess of Baden and some other guests in the pergola of the Villa San Michele. Munthe, on the left, turns away as usual from the camera. (1903)

The Crown Princess's companions on her walk, apart from the dogs, were her lady-in-waiting Cecilia Falkenberg and the chamberlain Jean Jacques De Geer. (1903)

Walks with the Crown Princess

The afternoons were usually spent as follows: at one o'clock, everyone met for lunch. Every day, after the Crown Princess had rested, she went for quite a long walk with myself and the chamberlain. She was receiving treatment for her eyes and had been prescribed a fair amount of exercise. Our route went first through the village past low, white houses with flat roofs or with high, white walls, and then on winding, rough paths up and down steep slopes. If we had not had Capri shoes of cloth with straw soles, this climbing would have been impossible. Vines, olives, figs, oranges, lemons, cactus and broom were growing here. Almond- and pear-trees in blossom could also be seen, together with well-tended patches of land with lupins. There were wild flowers in profusion.

Sometimes we met an old woman grazing her goat and young, often stately and handsome women with water jugs and other burdens on their heads. This is how manure and earth were carried up to the terrace-like vine-plantations! Almost everyone greeted us in a familiar fashion and looked up in wonder at the tall, elegant princess from the North. If the Crown Princess felt tired, then we stopped at one of our favourite spots in the vicinity, but otherwise the walk went on, sometimes to the westernmost tip of the island, sometimes to the steep slope under Anacapri, where one eventually reached the beach.

The tea hamper, which was always taken along on these afternoon walks, was entrusted to little »Lisa«, a genuine native of Capri, completely untouched by civilisation, with hair as black as coal, a dark-brown complexion, shining black eyes and regular features. The girl bore the hamper on her head, as is the custom of the country, and went on her way proud and untroubled. On one occasion we heard cries of distress from our little troop of followers, turned round fearfully and saw how the tea was pouring down over her head. The jug with the all-important drinks had burst!

Most enjoyable of all was discovering new, out-of-the-way places. Everywhere on this wonderful island was equally delightful. At about 5

While on her walks in Anacapri the Crown Princess wore her »Capri uniform« — a white costume of Capri wool, a straw hat and shoes with soles of plaited raffia. At picnics, the tea hamper was carried by a young girl, Lisa. (Photo Crown Princess Victoria 1903)

o'clock we took a longish break, and the tea was set out. It tasted good, I can promise you! Good use was made of the camera, and many of His Royal Highness's lovely photographs come from Capri.

If we had lost our way when so far afield, the road home could have been quite arduous, and on many occasions the Crown Princess's sure sense of direction was called for in order to find the right one among all those footpaths, deceptively similar to each other as they were.

Wherever we went during our walks we conscientiously destroyed the bird-snares which had been set with the intention of trapping the poor migratory birds returning home from the south: especially quail, which were popular with the hotel guests. The inhabitants of Capri are like all other south Italians: they have no sympathy for animals. Thus, little Lisa described how they would keep a live quail in a cage after putting out its eyes, for »it sings so prettily and serves as a decoy«. It was disturbing to hear the child quite cold-bloodedly describe something so horrible. The Crown Princess took great trouble to explain to the little savage how cruel both this and hunting generally were.

CECILIA AF KLERCKER (FALKENBERG), in her memoirs *Past Glory* (1944)

Munthe was camera-shy and only rarely allowed himself to be photographed from in front. During walks, Victoria had to photograph him more or less surreptitiously. The picture on the right shows Munthe at Torre della Guardia; the one on the left, beside the remains of another fortification in Anacapri. (1903)

During one of their walks the camera – possibly in the hands of Munthe – captured Victoria balancing on the edge of the abyss, presumably at Torre della Guardia. (1903?)

One of the first visitors to Munthe's villa was Marie Krøyer, who spent several months on Capri in the spring of 1896, when the building of the house had hardly begun. In June she was joined by her husband. They stayed on Capri for the rest of the summer. It was during this stay that Søren Krøyer made his fine pen drawing of Munthe the sailor.

Munthe was an inveterate sailor and enjoyed taking his guests cruising in the waters around Capri. In 1891 an English patient gave him a cutter which he named »Lady Victoria« after the daughter of the British ambassador in Rome, Lord Dufferin. »My beautiful cutter ›Lady Victoria‹ as as fine a boat as Scotland could build,« Munthe writes in The Story of San Michele, »teak and steel, ready for every emergency, safe in all weather if properly handled, and if ever I knew anything worth knowing it was how to steer a boat.« Here, the boat is anchored at Positano roads. (Photo Crown Princess Victoria, 1900?)

Prince Max of Baden and his wife Marie Louise celebrated their honeymoon on Capri in 1901. Their stay was immortalised in a photograph album which they presented to Munthe as a gift. The pictures show a jolly, smiling and laughing Munthe who for once did not shy from the camera. With the passing years Max and Munthe became close friends, united by common political and cultural interests. Sitting between the prince and Munthe is the royal couple's dog Lippo.

When Sweden's 22-year-old crown prince Gustaf Adolf came to Capri in March 1905 to introduce his fiancée Margaret to Victoria, Munthe let the prince, who was interested in archaeology, carry out excavations on pieces of land which belonged to him. »A malicious rumour had it,« Victoria's lady-in-waiting recalled, »that those artifacts that were found had been buried in advance by the prudent host.« (Photo Crown Princess Victoria)

The Animals

»In one respect at least I can say with a clear conscience that I have not de-
ceived my readers,« Munthe writes in *The Story of San Michele* – »in my love
for animals. I have loved them and suffered with them my whole life. I have
loved them far more than I have ever loved my fellow-men. All the best in me
I have given to them, and I mean to stand by them to the last and share their
fate whatever it may be.«

Munthe was a great dog-lover. His best known dog is Puck, a Great Dane
whose name he made part of his authorial identity by signing his books »Puck
Munthe«. Puck died during a walk in the Alps in 1888. Later, Munthe surrounded himself with many other dogs, as well as with monkeys and owls. And
during her stays in Capri The Crown Princess was accompanied by her poodles
Tom and Pussy, the lapponian shepherd Gioia and the fox-terrier Fellow.

One of the most hilarious characters in *The Story of San Michele* is the uncouth and alcoholic baboon Billy. The monkey which was captured by Crown Princess Victoria's camera is smaller in size, but it shared Billy's favourite occupation: catching the fleas on the doctor's dogs.

Munthe gave special consideration to the birds which rested on Capri every spring on their way from Africa to Scandinavia. »They came in thousands: woodpigeons, thrushes, turtle-doves, waders, quails, golden orioles, skylarks, nightingales, wagtails, chaffinches, swallows, warblers, redbreasts and many other tiny artists on their way to give spring concerts to the silent forests and fields in the North. A couple of hours later they fluttered helplessly in the nets the cunning of man had stretched all over the island from the cliffs by the sea high up to the slopes of Monte Solaro and Monte Barbarossa. In the evening they were packed by hundreds in small wooden boxes without food and water and despatched by steamers to Marseilles to be eaten with delight in the smart restaurants of Paris.«

When, in 1904, Munthe bought Mount Barbarossa, it was in order to turn at least this part of Capri into a haven for birds.

»In the little marble court outside the dining-room all ablaze with sun, sat Billy the baboon, hard at work catching Tappio's fleas, surrounded by all the other dogs drowsily awaiting their turn for the customary completion of their morning toilette. Billy had a wonderful hand for catching fleas, no jumping or crawling thing escaped his vigilant eye, the dogs knew it quite well and enjoyed the sport as much as he did.« (Photo Crown Princess Victoria, 1902?)

*The Russian greyhound Jal-
lah is bathed by two servant-girls under Munthe's
supervision. (Photo Crown
Princess Victoria 1902)*

Munthe in the cypress alley with his monkey. The fox-terrier is Victoria's Fellow. (Photo Crown Princess Victoria 1902)

Munthe at the Barbarossa fortress with, among others, Jallah, the lapponian shepherd Gioia, the Maremma dog Barbarossa and the fox-terrier Fellow. (1903?)

»Billy was afraid of nobody but me. I could always see by his face when he had a bad conscience which was generally the case. Yes, I think he was afraid of the mongoose who was always sneaking about the garden on restless feet, silent and inquisitive.«

The inquisitive mongoose is captured here by Crown Princess Victoria in San Michele's atrium. (1902?)

Victoria in company with the poodles Tom and Pussy in 1910, three years after she became queen of Sweden.

At the end of San Michele's pergola there is an outlook point where Victoria loved to sit. The plaques with the names of Victoria's dogs are not gravestones, as has sometimes been claimed — Tom and Fellow were still alive when the photograph was taken and were buried later under the cypresses at Materita, where Munthe had a dog cemetery. (Photo Crown Princess Victoria, 1901?)

*Munthe feeding a donkey.
(Photo Crown Princess
Victoria, 1902?)*

The Towers

The Villa San Michele was Munthe's permanent home for only a few years. In May 1902 he bought a medieval Saracen tower on the west side of the island, Torre di Materita, and from 1903 this was his principal dwelling. Munthe had had poor eyesight since childhood and was tormented by the strong sunlight on San Michele. Torre di Materita was in a more isolated location between the Caprile area of the town and the island's lighthouse, Faro, and the light there was less troublesome to his eyes. The tower was also considerably less damp than the Villa San Michele.

At about the same time as Munthe moved to Materita, he acquired two other medieval towers: Torre della Guardia, located close by, and Torre Dame-cuta on the north side of the island. He furnished La Guardia and rented it out to visiting friends. As for Damecuta, which stood on the ruins of an

imperial villa, it was surrounded by remains from antiquity which Munthe immediately began to excavate.

Crown Princess Victoria, who stayed on Capri almost every year, found it impractical in the long run to live in a hotel. To avoid the inconvenience she therefore decided to obtain a place of her own, and in 1906 she asked Munthe to help her buy a house and rebuild it to meet her requirements. Victoria wished to be as near her doctor as possible, and now that he was staying in Torre di Materita she chose a house on that part of the island. The house was situated on a west-facing slope in Caprile, a short walk from Munthe's tower. Casa Caprile was formally owned by Munthe until 1924, when it came into the queen's possession.

The panoramic picture on the previous double-spread, taken by Crown Princess Victoria, shows how isolated Torre di Materita was at the time Munthe acquired it. (1903)

The terrace and entrance to Torre di Materita.

From the roof of Materita there is an unobstructed view of Caprile, the western part of Anacapri. The large white house is Victoria's Casa Caprile.

Following double-spread: the prince and princess of Baden with Axel Munthe at Torre di Materita. The drawing was done by Baron Axel Gyllenstierna, Crown Princess Victoria's chamberlain during her stay in Capri in 1903.

The Swedish artist Anders Zorn visited Munthe at Materita at Easter 1912. »Yesterday at Munthe's on Capri – delightful,« he reported to his wife Emma: »One should really see him there. With rare good taste he has made the finest combination of architecture and ancient finds. Among the loveliest there is to see here. [...] Munthe obviously controls the greater part of the cultivated land in Capri and four villas.«

Prins Max v Baden
Prinsessan

Doktor Musette
Villa Materita 1905

The chapel at Materita with the Florentine stained-glass which, according to Munthe, he received as a present from the famous actress Eleonora Duse, and which at an earlier date had been positioned above the entrance to the chapel of the Villa San Michele.

Next double-spread: Axel Munthe photographed by Victoria at Torre della Guardia in 1903, the same year in which he acquired the tower and the land surrounding it. La Guardia was used mainly as a guesthouse. »I remember how he cherished his Guardia, his Saracen watchtower, and how he wanted no-one to know about it apart from a few peasants who lived nearby,« remembered Clare Frewen, Winston Churchill's cousin, who visited Capri in 1909: »The tower contained a furnished living-room filled with books and flowers and old Italian furniture, and a staircase led from this room through the ceiling up to my bedroom. It had a vaulted roof and the floor was inlaid with white tiles. The walls were whitewashed and a coloured porcelain madonna hung over the bed. The sun rose just opposite one of the windows and set just in front of the other. There was a delightfully spartan simplicity about the place, like in a convent.«

Torre Damecuta, which Munthe gifted to the Italian state in 1937 on the occasion of the 2,000th anniversary of the birth of the Emperor Augustus.

Casa Caprile as it looked at the beginning of the 20th century.

*Queen Victoria and her cousin Max at the entrance to
Casa Caprile 1912.*

It has been a Beautiful Day

LIKE CHILDREN in the trackless forest we grope our way through our lives in blissful ignorance of what is going to happen to us from one day to another, what hardships we may have to face, what more or less thrilling adventures we may encounter before the great adventure, the most thrilling of all, the Adventure of Death. Now and then in our perplexity we venture to put a timid question to our destiny, but we get no answer, for the stars are too far away. The sooner we realize that our fate lies in ourselves and not in the stars, so much the better for us. Happiness we can only find in ourselves, it is a waste of time to seek for it from others, few have any to spare. Sorrow we have to bear alone as best we can, it is not fair to try to shift it on others, be they men or women. We have to fight our own battles and strike as hard as we can, born fighters as we are.

Peace will come one day for all of us, peace without dishonour even to the vanquished if he has tried to do his bit as long as he could.

As for me, the battle is over and lost. I have been driven out of San Michele, the labour of a lifetime. I had built it stone by stone with my own hands in the sweat of my brow, I had built it on my knees to be a sanctuary-to the Sun where I was to seek knowledge and light from the glorious god I had been worshipping my whole life. I had been warned over and over again by the fire in my eyes that I was not worthy to live there, that my place was in the shade, but I had paid no heed to the warnings. Like the horses returning to their burning stables to perish in the flames, I had come back, summer after summer to the blinding light of San Michele. Beware of the light, beware of the light!

I have accepted my fate at last, I am too old to fight a god. I have retreated to my stronghold in the old tower where I mean to make a last stand. Dante was still alive when the monks set to work to build the Tower of Materita, half monastery, half fortress, strong as the rock it stands upon. How often has not his bitter cry of: »Nessun maggior dolore che ricordarsi del tempo felice nella miseria« echoed through its walls since

The sisters Rosina and Giovanninaa had been in service with Munthe since their teenage years. Giovannina (b. 1875?) emigrated to New Jersey in 1927, dying there in 1963, while Rosina (1877-1965) remained on Capri. In 1921 Rosina and her husband Enrico Massimino took over the running of the household at Torre di Materita. The family had eight children, including Vittorio. The photograph was taken at the end of the 1930s.

Vittorio Massimino, Rosina's son (b. 1912), worked as Munthe' assistant from his early years and accompanied him on journeys to England and Sweden. He is seen here escorting the half-blind Munthe on Capri in the spring of 1934.

I came here. But was he right after all, the Florentine seer? Is it true that there is no greater suffering than to remember our past happiness in our misery? I for one do not think so. It is with joy and not with sorrow that my thoughts go back to San Michele, where I have lived the happiest years of my life. But it is true I do not like to go there myself any more I feel as if I were intruding upon sacred ground, sacred to a past which can never return, when the world was young and the sun was my friend.

It is good to wander about in the soft light under the olives of Materita. It is good to sit and dream in the old tower, it is about the only thing I can do now. The tower looks towards the West, where the sun sets. Soon the sun will sink into the sea, then comes the twilight, then comes the night.

It has been a beautiful day.

AXEL MUNTHE, *The Story of San Michele*

Axel Munthe with his alsatian Gorm by the cypresses at Torre di Materita in the 1930s.

Nostalgia

Axel Munthe lived permanently on Capri for a good forty years, from 1901 until 1943. As long as Queen Victoria was alive, he seldom visited Sweden, but after her death in 1930 he was there every summer. In the autumn he returned to his beloved island, where he lived from October to May. But in September 1943 full-scale war was raging in southern Italy and Munthe remained in Sweden, where he had the use of three rooms in the Royal Palace in Stockholm.

Munthe suffered from the cold and the dark in his former homeland and dreamt of returning to Capri. As soon as the war was over, therefore, he began investigating how best to get there — by plane, boat or car? But he could not decide, and in any case he was far too frail for such a long and strenuous journey.

Munthe had been married since 1907 to an Englishwoman, Hilda Pennington-Mellor, by whom he had two sons; but he and his wife had separated in 1919, his relationship with the family was poor, and their contact with each other extremely sporadic. It was on Capri that he had had his real *famiglia* for the last half century: »I think about you the whole time and am very unhappy to be so far away from you all«, he wrote to Rosina in the autumn of 1945, adding: »Goodbye, dear Rosina, and all the family on Materita.«

Axcel Munthe was never to see the Villa San Michele or the Torre di Materita again. He died in the Royal Palace in Stockholm on 11th February 1949, in his 92nd year – 73 years after leaving Sweden in 1876.

In the spring of 1947 the Red Cross sister Karin Wiking used to keep Munthe company during his walks in Stockholm's Old Town. Munthe was as camera-shy as ever. But one day when Karin turned up with the dog Columbus, he let himself be persuaded. The photograph, taken by Karin Wiking in the courtyard of the Royal Palace, is the last known picture of Munthe.

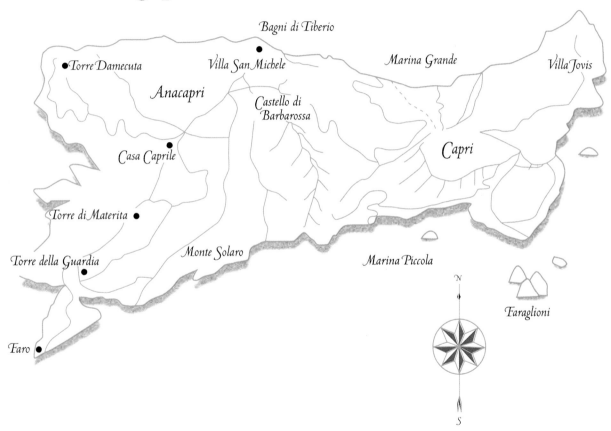

Capri

Bagni di Tiberio

Torre Damecuta

Villa San Michele

Marina Grande

Villa Jovis

Anacapri

Castello di
Barbarossa

Casa Caprile

Capri

Torre di Materita

Torre della Guardia

Monte Solaro

Marina Piccola

Faraglioni

Faro

N

S